BASIC IDIOMS IN ENGLISH

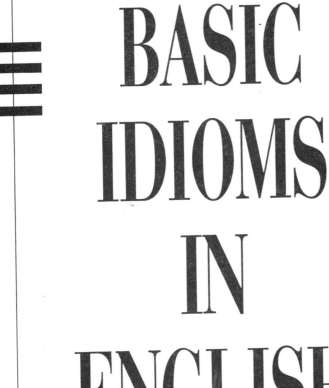

NEW EDITION • BOOK 1

HUBERT H. SETZLER, JR.

DOMINIE PRESS, INC.

Publisher: Raymond Yuen
Project Editor: Ronald E. Feare
Covers and Design: Gary Hamada
Illustrations: Sedonia Champlain
Audio Cassette Recordings: Laetitia Sonami

Published by
 Dominie Press, Inc.
5945 Pacific Center Boulevard
San Diego, California 92121 U.S.A.

ISBN 1-56270-098-7
Printed in U.S.A.
1 2 3 4 5 6 7 8 9 A 98 97 96 95 94 93

Preface

This is Book 1 of a four-book series entitled *Basic Idioms in English*.

These idioms have been selected for their frequent use by most Americans in their daily lives. Each lesson includes dialogues based on actual conversations – interviews – recorded by the author. These interviews accurately reflect the living language of Americans of all ages and walks of life.

Each of the books in the series is divided into five modules of four lessons each. Each lesson begins with a dialogue which introduces the new idioms in context. This is followed by an alphabetically-arranged listing of all new idioms with their respective definitions and two or more sample sentences. Then the student is asked to use those idioms in a variety of exercises.

Each module is a self-contained learning unit, that is, the student does not have to learn the first module in order to study the second one. The modules are independent. The same is true for the lessons. Teachers and learners of English can readily adapt the units to their own curriculum or individual needs.

Audio cassette recordings are available containing all dialogues and definitions of all idioms.

Table of Contents

Lesson **1**

How We See Things

Interview

The interviewer goes into Ted Lang's camera shop. He saw an advertisement in the newspaper for a new 35mm camera at Long's Camera World.

Int: Good morning, Ted. I saw your ad in the paper. I want to **see about** a new camera.

Ted: Fine. **Look at** this one. It's a great camera. It just came from Japan.

Int: Oh, yes. It's really nice. May I **take a picture?** I'd like to see how it works.

Ted: Sure, just **watch out for** the flash. You're looking right into it.

Int: I guess I don't know much about cameras. I'm going to **look to** you for advice.

Ted: Fine. I'll be glad to help.

Int: I also want to **shoot a video** of my family. Do you carry camcorders too?

Ted: We sure do. We have a wide selection.

1

Expressions

look at   *to examine, to watch*
The interviewer **looks at** a great camera from Japan.
Children are very curious. They **look at** everything.

look to   *to depend on, to rely on*
The interviewer **looks to** Ted for assistance in his
purchase.
Students **look to** their teacher for help with their
studies.

see about   *to investigate, to give*
                               attention or time to
The interviewer went to the store to **see about**
buying a new camera.
I don't have time to put gas in the car today. I'll **see
about** it tomorrow.

shoot a video   *to make a videotape*
                               by using a camcorder
The interviewer wants to buy a camcorder to **shoot a
video.**

I want to **shoot a video** of my son's fifth birthday next month.

take a picture of   *to photograph*
The interviewer doesn't know how to **take a picture** with a camera.
Quick! **Take a picture** of that beautiful sunset!

watch out for   *to guard against, to be careful of*
The interviewer has to **watch out for** the flash because he's looking right at it.
Watch out for that cat! It might scratch you.

EXERCISE 1

Match each idiom with its correct definition.

_____ 1. take a picture of   a. to examine

_____ 2. see about   b. to photograph

_____ 3. watch out for   c. to make a
                                       videotape

_____ 4. look to   d. to guard against

_____ 5. shoot a video   e. to give attention to

_____ 6. look at   f. to depend on

EXERCISE 2

Fill in each blank with the correct idiom. Each idiom is used only once.

takes a picture of	watch out for	look at
see about	looked to	shoots a video

1. Joe likes making videotapes. He _____ of almost everything.
2. Meg is a photographer. When she notices an interesting scene, she _____ it.
3. Johnny wants us to _____ him while he's riding his new bicycle.
4. When you cross the street, you must _____ speeding cars.
5. Mrs. Lee drove to the auto dealer to _____ buying a new car.
6. Mrs. Lee _____ the salesperson to give her good advice.

4

Lesson **2**

Asking for Advice

Interview

The interview is talking to Judy Davis, a travel agent, about his vacation plans.

Ms. Davis: What about the Riviera Coast of France? It's beautiful.

Int: Yes, I've **heard of** it. Would my wife and I **go in for** that area?

Ms. Davis: Yes, absolutely. My husband and I were there last year. We **talked about** the trip for weeks.

Int: Do you have information on special tours that I could look at?

Ms. Davis: Yes. We have several complete vacation packages. You should **speak to** our tour director.

Int: Yes, I'd like to **ask for** his advice also.

Ms. Davis: Fine. Just wait a minute. I'll ask him to **talk about** it with you.

Int: Yes, I would like to **listen to** him before I decide.

5

Expressions

ask for   *to request, to seek*
The interviewer **asks for** the advice of the tour director at the travel agency.
When you are lost, you can **ask for** advice from a policeman.

go in for   *to enjoy, to appreciate*
Ms. Davis and her husband really **went in for** the Riviera Coast.
Do you **go in for** reading a good book in bed at night?

hear of   *to know about,*
        to have knowledge of
The interviewer has **heard of** the Riviera Coast before.
Where is the Bering Strait? I've never **heard of** it.

listen to   *to pay attention to,*
                                     to consider

The interviewer wants to **listen to** the advice of the tour director.
Eric is in trouble. He didn't **listen to** his mother about playing with matches.

speak to   *to consult, to talk with*

The interviewer has to wait briefly before he can **speak to** the tour director.
You should **speak to** your supervisor about getting a better office.

talk about   *to discuss*

The interviewer and tour director **talk about** complete vacation packages.
Lynn and I **talked about** taking a camping trip in the summer.

EXERCISE 1

Match each idiom with its correct definition.

_____1. talk about	a. to pay attention to
_____ 2. listen to	b. to know about
_____ 3. go in for	c. to appreciate
_____ 4. ask for	d. to request
_____ 5. speak to	e. to discuss
_____ 6. hear of	f. to consult

EXERCISE 2

Fill in each blank with the correct idiom. Each idiom is used only once.

heard of	listens to	asked for
speak to	talk about	goes in for

1. Sarah plays tennis four times a week. She really _____ it.
2. Bill was very thirsty, so he _____a glass of water.
3. Who is Dr. Doe? I have never _____ him.
4. That boy is a real problem; he never _____ his parents.
5. I need my father's permission to buy a car, so I'll _____ him soon.
6. Sharon and Sue used to _____ movie stars all the time.

8

Lesson **3**

A Taste of Success

Interview

The interviewer is talking to Mrs. Turner about her young daughters, Kate and Meg.

Int: I heard that Kate wants to become an actress.

Mrs. Turner: Yes, Kate **had a taste of** acting in a commercial recently. It's too bad that Kate's become **stuck-up** as a result of the experience.

Int: I also heard that her sister Meg was in a school play this year.

Mrs. Turner: Yes, she was. Unfortunately, Meg had a bad experience during the play. Some children in the audience **laughed at** her.

Int: What happened? Did she suddenly get frightened on the stage?

Mrs. Turner: You hit it right **on the nose**. She couldn't even find the telephone she was supposed to answer, and it was right **under her nose**!

> **Int:** That's too bad.
>
> **Mrs. Turner:** Meg just couldn't **go on**. She ran right off the stage!

Expressions

go on	*to continue, to proceed*

Meg was unable to **go on** acting after she got stage fright during a school play.

I didn't mean to interrupt your conversation. Please **go on**.

have a taste of	*to have some experience with, to sample*

Recently Kate was in a commercial and **had a taste of** acting.

After Tony **had an** unpleasant **taste** of city life, he returned home to the country.

laugh at   *to ridicule, to scorn*
Some children in the audience **laughed at** Meg's
acting.
It's very unkind that you **laugh at** his mistakes like
that.

(right) on the nose   *exactly, precisely, accurately*
The interviewer hit it **right on the nose** about Meg's
stage fright.
I made a guess about her age and it was **on the nose**.

(right) under one's nose   *in an obvious place*
Meg didn't know that the telephone was **right under
her nose** on stage.
After an hour of searching, I finally found my car
keys **under my nose**.

stuck-up   *conceited, having an
                                exaggerated opinion of oneself*
Kate became somewhat **stuck-up** after she had a taste
of acting.
Now that Jake has won first prize in the talent
contest, he always seems **stuck-up**.

EXERCISE 1

Match each idiom with its correct definition.

_____ 1. have a taste of   a. conceited
_____ 2. right under one's nose   b. to continue
_____ 3. stuck-up   c. in an obvious
                                place
_____ 4. right on the nose   d. to sample
_____ 5. go on   e. accurately

EXERCISE 2

Fill in each blank with the correct idiom. Each idiom is used only once.

laughed at   had a taste of   on the nose
went on   stuck-up

1. Last year Jane _____ skiing for the first time.
2. She enjoyed it so much that she _____ skiing all day.
3. Sometimes she fell down, but no one _____ her.
4. Her best time down the ski slopes was 2 minutes _____.
5. Now that she is such a good skier, she is becoming a little _____ about her skills.

Lesson **4**

Think of the Cost

Interview

The interviewer is talking to Eric Gardner about his father's large new luxury car.

Int: What do you **think of** your father's new car?

Eric: I don't like it. I wanted him to buy one of those popular foreign cars, you know, a . . . well, the name just doesn't **come to mind** at the moment.

Int: Your father did **point out** that the price of his car was quite low.

Eric: Yes, but I **came up with** a different total cost.

Int: Oh, what's that?

Eric: I **figured out** that Dad could save over fifty dollars a month on gas if he bought a small compact car. That's a better way **in the long run.**

Int: Perhaps that's true, but obviously your father wanted a big, comfortable car!

13

Expressions

come to mind   *to be remembered*
The name of the foreign car that Eric prefers
doesn't come to mind.
If Marsha's telephone number **comes to mind**, let me
know immediately.

come up with   *to produce, to offer,*
                       to remember
Eric **came up with** a different overall cost for
operating a large car.
Sammy couldn't **come up with** an answer to the
teacher's question.
I can't **come up with** Marsha's telephone number
right now.

figure out   *to calculate, to solve,*
                       to understand
Eric **figured out** that his Dad could save a lot of
money in gas with a small car.
I tried to **figure out** the mathematics problem but it
was too difficult for me.

I can't **figure out** Jane. Usually she's nice but sometimes she can be unkind.

in the long run   *eventually,*
                             after a period of time
A small car would save a lot of money **in the long run**. **In the long run** it's better for your health to exercise and eat right.

point out   *to indicate,*
                             to bring to one's attention
Eric's Dad **pointed out** that the price of his new car was quite reasonable.
Let me **point out** that it was you who complained first, not I.

think of   *to have an opinion about*
Eric doesn't **think** highly **of** his father's new car because it's too big.
The company **thinks** a lot **of** their new sales program.

EXERCISE 1

Match each idiom with its correct definition.

_____ 1. come to mind   a. to have an opinion
                                      about
_____ 2. in the long run   b. to indicate
_____ 3. figure out   c. to produce
_____ 4. think of   d. to be remembered
_____ 5. point out   e. to calculate
_____ 6. come up with   f. eventually

EXERCISE 2

Fill in each blank with the correct idiom. Each idiom is used only once.

figure out	came to mind	pointed out
think of	came up with	in the long run

1. My father mentioned several of my faults, but he also _____ several of my good qualities.
2. My sister was able to _____ the algebra problem, but I was unable to solve it.
3. Some of my friends don't like my new suit. What do you _____ it?
4. Jim offered one possible solution to political disagreement, but Lenora _____ a better one.
5. I can't remember his address, but his telephone number just _____.
6. _____ you'll be glad that you worked so hard when you were young.

Module 1 Review

EXERCISE 1

Select the correct idiom for the boldface phrase.

1. **Examine** that sports car. What an unusual shape it has!
   a. Look to
   b. Look at
   c. Point out

2. **Be careful of** that dog. He might bite you.
   a. Watch out for
   b. See about
   c. Take a picture of

3. When you want to leave class early, you should **request** permission.
   a. call on
   b. ask for
   c. talk about

4. When you need advice, you should **pay attention to** your parents.
   a. listen to
   b. see about
   c. hear of

5. When you can't find the answer, you should **talk with** your teacher about it.
   a. talk about
   b. go in for
   c. speak to

6. I can't find my pen anywhere. Oh, here it is, **in an obvious place**.
   a. in the long run
   b. stuck-up
   c. right under my nose

7. Try not to **ridicule** his mistakes. He is doing his best.
   a. laugh at
   b. go in for
   c. ask for

8. After Chris **sampled** horseback riding, he wanted to do it often.
   a. talked about
   b. had a taste of
   c. went on

9. Most people are direct and sincere, but some are hard to **understand**.
   a. figure out
   b. come to mind
   c. point out

10. Perhaps later I will be able to **remember** her name.
    a. come up with
    b. think about
    c. hear of

EXERCISE 2

Fill in the boxes of the crossword puzzle with the correct idioms.

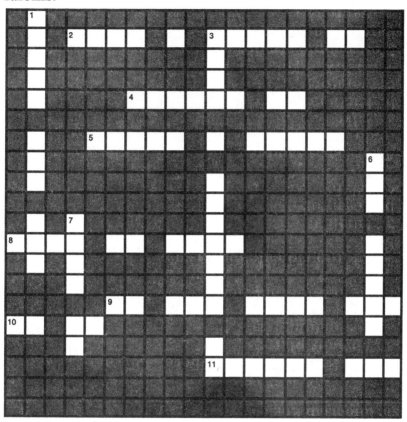

Across
2. have some experience with, sample
4. pay attention to, consider
5. make a videotape by using a camcorder
8. produce, offer, remember
9. eventually, after a period of time
10. continue, proceed
11. calculate, solve, understand

Down
1. guard against, be careful of
3. photograph
6. investigate, give attention or time to
7. know about, have knowlege of

19

Lesson **1**

Meeting Others Halfway

Interview

The inverviewer is talking to Ed Burns, a salesman for Kingman Real Estate. He and his boss, Mike Kingman, are trying to sell a new home to Mrs. Livingston.

Ed: I can only talk with you a few minutes. Mike and I have to **call on** Mrs. Livingston soon.

Int: Is Mike Kingman your boss, Mr. Burns?

Ed: Yes, he insists that I **call** him **by his first name**.

Int: The two of you must work closely together.

Ed: Yes. Today we're going to sell Mrs. Livingston a new house. Last week she **came up to** Mike in the office and asked about the price of our homes.

Int: Do you know Mrs. Livingston well?

Ed: No, I only **know** her **by sight**. Mike is a friend of hers, though.

Int: This should be an easy sale, then.

20

Ed: No, she already thinks that the price is too high. When she sees the inside of the house, I think that it will **come up to** her expectations.

Int: What if she still thinks that the price is too high?

Ed: Then we'll compromise with her. We'll have to **meet** her **halfway**.

Expressions

---

call on   *to visit*
Ed Burns and Mike Kingman will **call on** Mrs. Livingston soon.
We shouldn't **call on** the Masons now because it's getting too late.

call by (one's) first name   *to use a given (first) name instead of a title name such as Mr. or Mrs. and the last name*

Mr. Kingman wants Ed Burns to **call** him **by** his **first name**.
Americans usually **call** other people **by** their **first names**.

come up to   *to approach closely; to match, to equal*
Mrs. Livingston **came up to** Mike in the office and asked about a new home.
The new home will probably **come up to** Mrs. Livingston's expectations.

know by sight   *to recognize by appearance only*
Ed Burns only **knows** Mrs. Livingston **by sight**; he's never been introduced to her.
I never met the president of the company, but I **know** him **by sight**.

meet halfway   *to compromise with*
Ed and Mike are willing to **meet** Mrs. Livingston **halfway** on the selling price.
We could stop arguing if you would just **meet** me **halfway**.

EXERCISE 1

Match each idiom with its correct definition.

_____ 1. come up to	a. to compromise with
_____ 2. call on	b. to visit
_____ 3. meet halfway	c. to recognize by appearance only
_____ 4. know by sight	d. to approach closely
_____ 5. call by one's first name	e. to use a given name

EXERCISE 2

Fill in each blank with the correct idiom. Each idiom is used only once.

call you by your first name   call on
know . . . by sight   come up to
meet . . . halfway

1. First let's visit my parents, and then we can
   _____ your parents.
2. It's nice to meet you. If you call me Hugh, I'll
   _____.
3. I know Mr. Watanabe very well, but I
   _____ Mr. Yamada only _____.
4. He'll compromise with you, if you're willing to
   _____ him _____.
5. That salesman approached me about buying a
   new suit. Did he also_____ you?

Lesson **2**

Getting Along with Others

Interview

The interview is talking to Audra Dixon, a ten-year-old school girl, about her new music teacher, Ms. Davis.

Int: How do you **get along with** your new music teacher?

Audra: Ms. Davis? She's wonderful. She really makes me feel **at ease**.

Int: I hear that she's a good teacher.

Audra: Yes. She loves music and teaches it well. All of her students **look up to** her greatly.

Int: I also hear that she's very strict.

Audra: That's right. She makes you learn all the music **by heart**.

Int: That must be difficult for you.

Audra: Yes, but after a while you **get used to** it.

Expressions

---

get along with *to live or work well with someone*

Audra **gets along** well **with** her new music teacher.

How are you **getting along with** your roommate?

at ease *comfortable, relaxed*

Ms. Davis makes Audra feel **at ease** during the music lessons.

Mike didn't feel **at ease** standing in front of such a large audience.

look up to *to respect, to admire*

All of the music students **look up to** Ms. Davis as a fine teacher.

Marsha **looks up to** both of her parents for all the help they've given her.

by heart *by memorizing completely*

Ms. Davis' students have to learn each piece of music **by heart**.

The politician learned his speech **by heart** before the election campaign.

get used to   *to gradually accept or*
                         become familiar with

Audra has **gotten used to** learning all of her music by heart.

It's often difficult to **get used to** the food when you travel to another country.

EXERCISE 1

Match each idiom with its correct definition.

_____ 1. at ease   a. to respect

_____ 2. look up to   b. by memorizing
                                completely

_____ 3. by heart   c. to gradually accept

_____ 4. get used to   d. to live or work well
                                with

_____ 5. get along with   e. comfortable,
                                relaxed

EXERCISE 2

Fill in each blank with the correct idiom. Each idiom is used only once.

get used to   look up to   get along with
at ease   by heart

1. Lisa doesn't think that she can ever _____ cold weather.

2. A teacher who works hard and prepares well for class is someone that you can _____.

3. Luisa tried to learn the vocabulary list _____, but there were too many words to remember.

4. Brett and Elizabeth are very good friends. Elizabeth and Brett _____ each other well.

5. I feel so much _____ when I find a quiet place to study in the library.

Lesson **3**

You'll Get over It

Interview

The interviewer is talking to Ken Morris, a senior in high school. He and his girlfriend Elizabeth have just ended their relationship.

Int: So you **broke up with** Elizabeth.

Ken: Yes. But I miss her a lot. I just can't **get over** losing her.

Int: How long did you date Elizabeth?

Ken: I **went with** her for over two years.

Int: That's a long time for high school students. You must have loved her.

Ken: Yes, I did. Right now I'm afraid of getting hurt again.

Int: I understand. **I fell for** someone when I was in high school.

Ken: I assume that the two of you **broke up** too. Did it take you a long time to get over her?

Int: Yes, it did. However, I found someone who hasn't **let** me **down** in life, and so will you!

27

Expressions

break up (with)	*to end a relationship with someone*

It was difficult for Ken **to break up with** Elizabeth.
A couple stops dating when their relationship **breaks up**.

fall for	*to become in love with; to be fooled or tricked by*

The interviewer, like Ken, **fell for** a girl while he was in high school.
The teacher didn't **fall for** the excuse that the student gave for being late.

get over	*to recover from (an illness or emotional problem)*

Ken is still unable to **get over** losing his girlfriend.
It took Cindy a long time to **get over** that bad cold she had.

go with   *to date regularly;*
                         to accompany
Ken **went with** Elizabeth in high school for over two years.
Would you like to **go with** me to the shopping center?

let down   *to disappoint, to fail to*
                         meet one's expectations
Some day Ken will meet someone who won't **let** him **down**.
Lisa **let** her parents **down** when she failed to get passing grades in school.

EXERCISE 1

Match each idiom with its correct definition.

_____ 1. break up with   a. to date regularly

_____ 2. get over   b. to disappoint

_____ 3. go with   c. to recover from

_____ 4. fall for   d. to become in love
                                         with

_____ 5. let down   e. to end a
                                         relationship with

EXERCISE 2

Fill in each blank with the correct idiom. Each idiom is used only once.

going with him	let her down	getting over
fall for it	break up with	

1. Patty really enjoys dating Sam. She has been _____ for several months.
2. Deborah trusts Thomas completely. She's certain that he will never _____.
3. Frank and Nancy decided to _____ each other because they had almost no common interests.
4. When the criminal used the excuse that he was at home all night, the police didn't _____.
5. Robert has had difficulty _____ the death of his parents.

Lesson **4**

Don't Give Up

Interview

The interviewer is talking to Molly Hughes, who has recently finished college and is now deciding on her career.

Int: What are you going to do, Molly, now that your college days **are over**?

Molly: I don't know. I had to **give up** my hope of becoming a scientist like my Mom and Dad wanted.

Int: Why is that?

Molly: My grades in science weren't high enough. I couldn't **live up to** the goals I set for myself.

Int: You did well in college. I'm sure you **lived up to** your parents' expectations.

Molly: I hope so. I wish they'd tell me **face to face** how they really feel.

Int: Why don't you tell them what you'd like to be?

31

Molly: I should. I **used to** want to be a teacher. I think my parents would like that.

Int: It's important for you and your parents to understand each other.

Molly: Yes, you're right.

Expressions

---

be over   *to be completed or finished*
Molly's college days **are over** and she is now deciding on a career.
This movie is so boring that I hope it**'s over** soon.

face to face   *directly, personally*
Molly wishes that her parents would tell her **face to face** how they feel.
My boss and I met **face to face** to discuss problems with the new employees.

give up   *to surrender, to stop*
                               (a bad habit)
Molly had to **give up** her hope of ever becoming a
scientist.
Some people try to **give up** smoking but never
succeed.

live up to   *to fulfill, to meet one's*
                               expected standards
Molly isn't certain that she is **living up to** her
parents' expectations.
Tanya is an excellent worker because she **lives up to**
her responsibilities.

used to   *had the habit or custom to*
Molly **used to** want to be a teacher, and she thinks
her parents would like it.
Someone who has given up cigarettes **used to** smoke
but doesn't anymore.

EXERCISE 1

Match each idiom with its correct definition.

_____ 1. give up   a. had the habit or
                                 custom to

_____ 2. live up to   b. to surrender

_____ 3. face to face   c. directly, personally

_____ 4. used to   d. to fulfill

_____ 5. be over   e. to be completed or
                                 finished

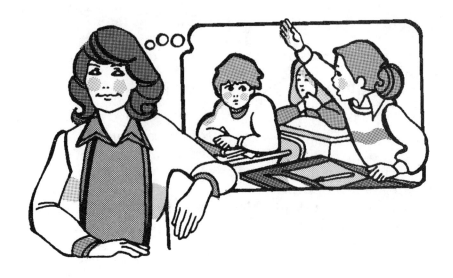

EXERCISE 2

Fill in each blank with the correct idiom. Each idiom is used only once.

was over   face to face   give up
live up to   used to

1. English is a difficult language, but don't
   _____ trying to learn it.
2. The large party _____ at around one
   o'clock in the morning.
3. Frederick and Teresa met _____ to discuss
   their failing marriage.
4. Antonio couldn't _____ his parents'
   expectation that he would become a doctor.
5. I _____ date Charles regularly, but now I
   have a new boyfriend.

Module 2 Review

EXERCISE 1

Select the correct idiom for the boldface phrase.

1. Did he say that you could **use his given name**?
   a. know him by sight
   b. call him by his first name
   c. call on him

2. Children should be careful when strangers
   approach them closely on the streets.
   a. come up to them
   b. meet them halfway
   c. know them by sight

3. When is a good time for us to **visit you** this
   evening?
   a. look up to you
   b. call on you
   c. be over you

4. After a difficult first semester in school, Barbara
   is **gradually becoming familiar with** working hard.
   a. knowing by sight about
   b. living up to
   c. getting used to

5. I enjoy talking with Michelle because she makes
   me feel completely **relaxed**.
   a. face to face
   b. at ease
   c. by heart

6. When Todd didn't help Karla with arrangements for the party, he really **disappointed her**.
   a. met her halfway
   b. fell for her
   c. let her down

7. It took Phil two weeks to **recover from** a bad case of influenza.
   a. call on
   b. break up
   c. get over

8. Jake prefers **regularly dating** one girl rather than several at one time.
   a. falling for
   b. going with
   c. breaking up with

9. Matthew was forced to **stop** drinking when he had trouble with his stomach.
   a. be over
   b. fall for
   c. give up

10. The children in the Simpson family **fulfill** their obligations by doing daily chores around the house.
    a. live up to
    b. get used to
    c. look up to

EXERCISE 2

Fill in the boxes of the crossword puzzle with the correct idioms.

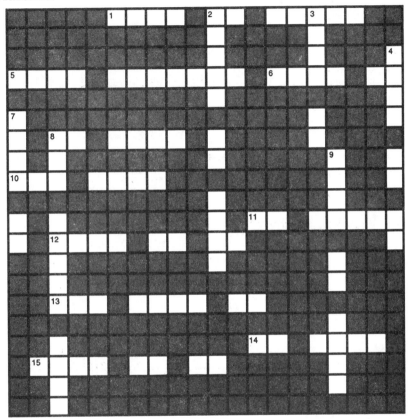

Across
1. recognize by appearance
5. compromise
6. had the habit or custom to
8. disappoint
11. by memorizing completely
12. respect, admire
13. gradually accept
14. comfortable, relaxed
15. fulfill, meet a standard

8. *dating*

10

Down
2. end a relationship with
3. surrender, stop a habit
4. approach closely
7. visit
8. live or work well with
9. personally, directly

Lesson **1**

A Good Time

Interview

The interviewer is talking with Jim Marshall, a TV game show host.

Int:	The contestants on your game show must be interesting people.
Marshall:	Well, yes, they are. **At times** we have trouble with them, though.
Int:	Oh? What kind of trouble?
Marshall:	Usually they get very nervous. **Time and time again** I have to tell them to relax and **have a good time**.
Int:	Do they listen to you?
Marshall:	Unfortunately, it doesn't **do** much **good**. They just get more **on edge**!
Int:	Do you enjoy hosting the show?
Marshall:	**For the time being** I enjoy it. I've already come up with some interesting ideas for a new show, though.
Int:	Good luck!

Expressions

at times *sometimes, occasionally*
At times Mr. Marshall has trouble with the game show contestants.
At times Kathy goes out of town on a business trip.

do good *to benefit, to help (used with much and any)*
It doesn't **do** much **good** for Mr. Marshall to tell the contestants to relax.
Did it **do** any **good** for you to speak to your teacher about the bad grade?

for the time being *temporarily, during the present time*
For the time being Mr. Marshall enjoys hosting the game show.
We're living in an apartment **for the time being**, but we'd prefer a house.

have a good time *to enjoy oneself (often used with relax and . . .)*

Mr. Marshall tells the contestants to relax and **have a good time**.
Forget about work. Let's go out to dinner and just **have a good time**.

on edge   *nervous, anxious, concerned*
Many of the contestants get more **on edge** as the show goes on.
Some people feel at ease in front of audiences and others feel **on edge**.

time and time again   *repeatedly, frequently*
Time and time again Mr. Marshall tries to get the contestants to relax.
I had to remind my son **time and time again** to finish his homework after school.

EXERCISE 1

Match each idiom with its correct definition.

_____ 1. on edge   a. repeatedly, frequently

_____ 2. at times   b. to enjoy oneself

_____ 3. do good   c. temporarily

_____ 4. have a good time   d. occasionally

_____ 5. for the time being   e. nervous, anxious

_____ 6. time and time again   f. to benefit, to help

EXERCISE 2

Fill in each blank with the correct idiom. Each idiom is used only once.

at times   doing you good
having a good time   time and time again
for the time being   on edge

1. If you practice that song _____, you'll learn it quickly.
2. This beach party is fun. I'm _____.
3. It's not _____ to stay up so late and to get so little sleep.
4. I don't enjoy this job, but _____ I'll have to keep it.
5. The new TV newsman looked _____ in front of the camera.
6. _____ Mr. Curto likes to take his truck camper on a weekend trip.

Lesson **2**

Quit Smoking for Good

Interview

The interviewer is talking with his friend, Pete Vincent, about his bad smoking habit. Pete is a busy insurance agent who smokes constantly.

Int: Why do you smoke, Pete?

Pete: I smoke because smoking relaxes me.

Int: It relaxes you?

Pete: Yes, it does. Life is so hectic. Everyone's **in a hurry**. Everything is rush, rush, rush. So I relax by having a cup of coffee and a cigarette.

Int: I've suggested **over and over** that you stop. Cigarettes can ruin your health.

Pete: I know. **As usual**, I don't listen to you.

Int: Do you think you'll ever quit?

Pete: I hope so. **Little by little** I'm smoking less every day.

Int: That's great, Pete! Soon you'll be able to quit smoking **for good**.

42

Expressions

---

as usual   *customarily, as is typical*
As usual, Pete Vincent doesn't listen to advice about his smoking habit.
Juanita received high marks in school **as usual**.

for good   *permanently, forever*
Some day Pete wants to give up smoking **for good**.
Kate has decided to break up with her boyfriend **for good**.

in a hurry   *hurried, rushed*
Pete thinks that life is hectic because everyone around him is **in a hurry**.
I had to eat my breakfast **in a hurry** because I was almost late for school.

little by little   *gradually*
Little by little Pete is smoking fewer cigarettes each day.
The sad story of life is that we are all growing older **little by little**.

over and over (again)   *repeatedly*
The interviewer has suggested **over and over again**
that Pete stop smoking.
Over and over the child opened and shut the door
to the kitchen.

EXERCISE 1

Match each idiom with its correct definition.

_____ 1. little by little   a. repeatedly
_____ 2. in a hurry   b. gradually
_____ 3. over and over again c. hurried, rushed
_____ 4. for good   d. permanently,
                                          forever
_____ 5. as usual   e. customarily

EXERCISE 2

Fill in each blank with the correct idiom. Each idiom is used only once.

as usual   for good   in a hurry
little by little   over and over

1. Mr. Wilson is late to work this morning _____. He almost never arrives at the right time.

2. The children ran home _____ because the big storm was getting closer each minute.

3. We used to be able to hold our two young boys, but _____ they are getting too big to hold anymore.

4. In order to learn these difficult vocabulary words for tomorrow's test, you'll have to study them _____.

5. Coffee really makes me feel on edge. I want to quit drinking coffee _____.

Lesson **3**

It's Time to Learn to Ski

Interview

The interviewer is talking to Pat Hale about his skiing experiences.

Int: How do you like skiing, Pat?

Pat: I love it. **All my life** I've wanted to learn. Finally I took lessons last year.

Int: I suppose skiing is easy for you.

Pat: No, sir! **At first** I couldn't even get up on my skis. Next I fell down **from time to time**. Then **all of a sudden** I started skiing much better.

Int: I see. Do you ski often?
Pat: Every chance I get. On some weekends I ski **all day long**.

Int: That sounds great.

Pat: Why don't you learn how to ski?

Int: **Not on your life!** I'd break my leg!

Expressions

all day long	*throughout the entire day (other time periods, such as week, month, year, may be used)*

On some weekends Pat goes skiing **all day long**.
All week long the weather has been cold and rainy.

all of a sudden	*suddenly*

All of a sudden Pat discovered that he could ski much better.
We were driving down the highway when, **all of a sudden**, the engine failed.

all (one's) life	*during one's entire lifetime*

Pat has wanted to learn how to ski **all his life**.
All my life I've lived in the same city and had the same job.

at first   *in the beginning, initially*
Pat couldn't even stand up on his skis **at first**.
At first American food was strange to Yuki, but then
she got used to it.

not on your life   *absolutely not, definitely not*
When asked about learning to ski, the interviewer
responds, "**Not on your life!**"
Not on your life would I buy that old car from you.

from time to time   *sometimes, occasionally*
Pat would fall down **from time to time** while he was
skiing.
From time to time Connie stops by to visit her
parents.

EXERCISE 1

Match each idiom with its correct definition.

_____ 1. all day long   a. in the beginning
_____ 2. at first   b. suddenly
_____ 3. all one's life   c. throughout the
                                    entire day
_____ 4. all of a sudden   d. sometimes
_____ 5. not on your life   e. during one's
                                    entire lifetime
_____ 6. from time to time   f. absolutely not

EXERCISE 2

Fill in each blank with the correct idiom. Each idiom is used only once.

all her life   all of a sudden   all week long
from time to time   not on your life   at first

1. _____ would I skydive out of an airplane
   with you!
2. Audrey is in Paris for the first time now. She has
   wanted to visit there _____.
3. Most of the time Michael reads or works in the
   evening, but _____ he watches TV.
4. _____ an earthquake shook the ground
   and all the buildings.
5. Bob stayed home in bed with a bad cold
   _____.
6. _____ I was afraid to go on the fast new
   rollercoaster, but then I agreed to try it.

Lesson **4**

Going to School

Interview

The interview is talking to Mrs. Neel, a middle-aged woman who goes to college.

Int:	How do you feel about **going to school** after so long?
Mrs. Neel:	I love it. I always wanted to **go to college** when I was younger.
Int:	Why didn't you go to college then?
Mrs. Neel:	Oh, the usual reasons. **In no time** Dave and I decided to get married, and then I had to **bring up** two children.
Int:	I see. How did your children feel when you started college?
Mrs. Neel:	They thought it was great. **Now and then** I felt uncertain but they encouraged me. They even **made room for** my desk in their study room.
Int:	Did it scare you a little to go back to school?

Mrs. Neel: Yes. At first I couldn't ask or answer questions in class. Sometimes I couldn't wait until the class time **was up**. Now I really enjoy it!

Expressions

be up	*to be expired, to be finished (for time only)*

Mrs. Neel was often on edge in class and wished that the time **was up**.

The students stopped taking the test when the 30 minutes **were up**.

bring up	*to rear, to raise from childhood*

Mrs. Neel couldn't go to school because she had to **bring up** two children.

I look up to my parents because they **brought** me **up** well.

go to school or college	*to attend school or college*

Mrs. Neel couldn't **go to college** until later in her life.

51

Mr. Yamamoto and Mr. Osawa **went to school** at the same time.

in no time   *very quickly, rapidly*
After high school, Mrs. Neel got married **in no time** and had children.
In no time George dressed, ate breakfast, and left for work.

make room for   *to create space for,*
                                                      to accommodate
Mrs. Neel's children **made room for** her desk in their study room.
Could you move over and **make room for** me on the couch?

now and then   *sometimes, occasionally*
Now and then Mrs. Neel felt uncertain about returning to college.
Please stir the noodles in the saucepan **now and then**.

EXERCISE 1

Match each idiom with its correct definition.

_____	1. make room for	a. very quickly, rapidly
_____	2. in no time	b. to attend school
_____	3. now and then	c. to create space for
_____	4. be up	d. to be expired
_____	5. bring up	e. occasionally
_____	6. go to school	f. to raise from childhood

EXERCISE 2

Fill in each blank with the correct idiom. Each idiom is used only once.

was up	bringing up	going to college
make room for	in no time	now and then

1. I think we can _____ one more person in the back seat of the car.

2. Karl decided to get a job instead of _____

3. _____ the firemen were able to stop the grass fire near some valuable homes.

4. Our family had fun _____ two kittens named Minu and Blacky.

5. _____ my wife and I will eat dinner by candlelight.

6. When the teacher said that the time _____, many students still hadn't finished the exam.

Module 3 Review

EXERCISE 1

Select the correct idiom for the boldface phrase.

1. It will **benefit you** to lose weight and start exercising more.
   a. have a good time
   b. do you good
   c. make room for you

2. We have to use a rental car **temporarily** while our own car is being fixed.
   a. time and time again
   b. at times
   c. for the time being

3. Steve was really **nervous** before an important job interview.
   a. having a bad time
   b. on edge
   c. brought up

4. I woke up at seven o'clock in the morning **as is typical**.
   a. for good
   b. as usual
   c. over and over

5. **Repeatedly** the student gave the same response to the teacher's question.
   a. In a hurry
   b. Little by little
   c. Over and over

6. **Gradually** the long train increased its speed out of the station.
   a. Little by little
   b. Time and time again
   c. In a hurry

7. Marie has wanted to become a movie star **during her entire life**.
   a. not on her life
   b. all her life
   c. all year long

8. **Throughout the entire night** Terry was awake with a fever and bad cough.
   a. All night long
   b. All of a sudden
   c. From time to time

9. **Occasionally** Tina likes to eat a large chocolate ice cream sundae.
   a. Now and then
   b. In no time
   c. All of a sudden

10. Lee was so hungry that he ate dinner **very quickly**.
   a. all of a sudden
   b. in no time
   c. time and time again

EXERCISE 2

Fill in the boxes of the crossword puzzle with the correct idioms.

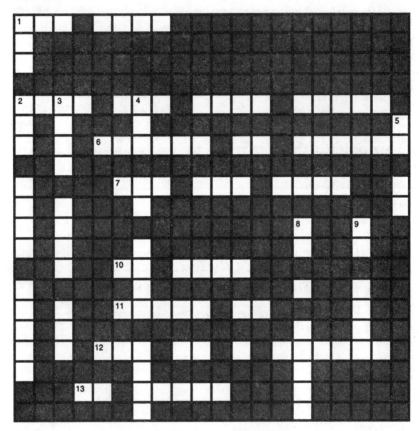

Across
1. permanently, forever
2. repeatedly, frequently
6. gradually
7. sometimes, occasionally
10. benefit, help
11. raise, rear
12. suddenly
13. in the beginning

Down
1. temporarily
3. create space for, accommodate
4. absolutely not
5. be expired, be finished
8. rushed, hurried
9. nervous, anxious

Lesson **1**

Keep on Trying

Interview

The interviewer is talking to Gloria Bingham, a college student.

Int: Were you able **to talk** your father **into** buying you a car?

Gloria: Well, I **was about to** speak to him this afternoon, but he didn't return home until later.

Int: Why?

Gloria: You won't believe this! He was going to return at one o'clock, but his car **broke down** on the highway.

Int: That's not a good time to talk to him about a car.

Gloria: Absolutely. I've decided to **put off** talking to him until next week.

Int: What if he never agrees to buy one?

Gloria: I'm never giving up! I'll **keep on** talking to him about that car until he agrees.

Expressions

be about to	*to be ready or prepared to do something*

Gloria **was about to** discuss getting a car with her father that afternoon.

James and Myra **were about to** leave the house when the phone rang.

break down	*to fail to operate, to stop functioning*

Gloria's father was late returning home because his car **broke down**.

If this typewriter **breaks down**, I'll be unable to complete my class assignment.

keep on	*to continue*

Gloria will **keep on** talking to her father until he agrees to buy a car.

The children **kept on** playing outside even after it started to rain.

put off   *to postpone, to delay*
Gloria will **put off** talking to her father until next week.
The director couldn't attend the meeting, so she **put** it **off** for two days.

to talk into   *to convince about,*
                                     to persuade about
Gloria is going to **talk** her father **into** buying a car for her.
You can't **talk** me **into** going with you; I'm not interested in opera.

EXERCISE 1

Match each idiom with its correct definition.

_____ 1. break down   a. to convince, to
                                  persuade about

_____ 2. talk into   b. to be ready or
                                  prepared to

_____ 3. put off   c. to continue

_____ 4. keep on   d. to postpone, to
                                  delay

_____ 5. be about to   e. to fail to operate

EXERCISE 2

Fill in each blank with the correct idiom. Each idiom is used only once.

was about to	broke down	keep on
put it off	talk her into	

1. The students weren't ready for the exam, so the professor _____ until the following week.
2. I _____ eat lunch when the doorbell rang.

3. We tried to _____ riding the rollercoaster, but she refused.
4. Just after she refused to ride the rollercoaster, it _____.

5. Bill wants to _____ learning Spanish as long as possible.

Lesson **2**

Getting Rid of a Problem

Interview

The interviewer is talking to Mrs. Salt, a housewife, about her common household problems.

Mrs. Salt: Sometimes I hate to **keep house**.

Int: Why is that? Don't your husband and children **help out**?

Mrs. Salt: No, they're not much help. Actually, they **hang on to** so much junk that I can't stand it. I try to **get rid of** old stuff all the time.

Int: Won't they let you **throw** it **away** when it gets too old?

Mrs. Salt: No, they won't! It's too important to them.

Int: When I was young, I liked to collect things too.

Mrs. Salt: So did I. But look at this. My son keeps his old tennis shoes even after he has **worn** them **out**!

61

Expressions

get rid of *to eliminate, to sell*

Mrs. Salt often wants **to get rid of** unnecessary items around the house.

I'll have **to get rid of** my car if I don't find a job soon.

hang on to *to keep, not to sell or eliminate*

Mrs. Salt's husband and children **hang on to** all their old stuff for too long.

Mike is **hanging on to** his old glasses in case his new ones ever break.

help out *to assist, to aid*

Mrs. Salt's husband and children don't often **help out** with chores at home.

I was grateful when my friends **helped** me **out** with moving to a new place.

keep house   *to do the necessary work*
                             in a house
Mrs. Salt sometimes hates to **keep house** because she doesn't get much help.
Some families are able to hire maids to **keep house** for them.

throw away   *to discard*
Mrs. Salt's husband and children never **throw away** anything important to them.
Instead of **throwing away** that food, why don't you feed it to the dog?

wear out   *to make or become*
                             unusable through wear
Mrs. Salt's son even keeps his tennis shoes after he has **worn** them **out**.
If your shoes are **worn out**, you should throw them away.

EXERCISE 1

Match each idiom with its correct definition.

_____ 1. throw away   a. to make or become
                                  unusable

_____ 2. keep house   b. to discard

_____ 3. help out   c. to do the necessary
                                  housework

_____ 4. hang on to   d. to assist, to aid

_____ 5. wear out   e. to eliminate, to
                                  sell

_____ 6. get rid of   f. to keep, not to sell

EXERCISE 2

Fill in each blank with the correct idiom. Each idiom is used only once.

get rid of	hang on to	help out
keep house	throw away	wore out

1. You have to _____ that big car. It uses too much gas.
2. I should really _____ this old sweater. It's in terrible condition.
3. In many countries, it is expected that men will help women to _____.
4. When a friend is in trouble, you should always _____.
5. When I buy something, I always _____ the receipt for the purchase.
6. Zachary got new tires for his bicycle when the old ones _____.

Lesson **3**

Coming Back Home

Interview

The interviewer is talking to an old friend, John Eggert, who must travel a great deal on business.

Int: Hello, John. It's good to see you. When did you **get home**?

John: I arrived at the airport this afternoon. My wife **picked** me **up**.

Int: I know that your children must be glad to see you after another long trip.

John: Yes, they missed me a lot. They couldn't wait for me to **be back** home.

Int: Say, John, there's a party at the Hale's house tomorrow night. Would you and Nancy like to **come along with** us?

John: Oh, thanks, John, but it's not possible this weekend. I have to **be back** to work in Washington in a few days.

Int: **Of course.** I understand. We'll **get together** another time.

Expressions

be back   *to return somewhere*
John's children couldn't wait for him to **be back** home.
When are you going to **be back** this evening?

come along with   *to accompany*
The interviewer invites John and Nancy to **come along with** him to a party.
Would Derek enjoy **coming along with** us to the park?

get home   *to arrive home*
John **got home** in the afternoon from travelling on business.
Sally always **gets home** at about the same time each evening.

get together   *to meet socially*
The interviewer and John will **get together** at a later time.

If you're available, we can **get together** at around 9 p.m. tonight.

of course   *certainly, naturally*
Of course the interviewer understands that John and Nancy are not available.
I'd much rather be rich than poor, **of course**.

pick up   *to meet for the purpose of transporting*
John's wife **picked** him **up** at the airport in the afternoon.
Would you mind **picking** me **up** at my office on your way home?

EXERCISE 1

Match each idiom with its correct definition.

_____ 1. get together   a. naturally, certainly

_____ 2. get home   b. to meet socially

_____ 3. come along with   c. to meet to transport

_____ 4. be back   d. to arrive home

_____ 5. pick up   e. to return somewhere

_____ 6. of course   f. to accompany

EXERCISE 2

Fill in each blank with the correct idiom. Each idiom is used only once.

be back	come along with	got home
got together	of course	pick up

1. Mr. Dern worked late at the office yesterday, but he _____ in time for dinner.
2. When will you _____ from the doctor's office?
3. Faye was busy so she couldn't _____ us to the zoo.
4. What time are we going to _____ your parents at the airport?
5. The Jensens _____ with their neighbors for coffee and dessert.
6. _____ I would accept a million dollars if I won it in a contest!

Lesson **4**

Tired Out

Interview

The interview is talking to Phil Rambow, a very active member of the community.

Int: Phil, you really look **tired out**. Did you have a busy day?

Phil: I certainly did. I could **fall asleep** right here in the office.

Int: Why don't you **lie down** on the couch then?

Phil: I'd love to, but I have a conference in thirty minutes and a city government meeting after work.

Int: Well, at least you can **sit down** for a while.

Phil: I guess I should. Please **take a seat** too.

Int: Phil, you just do too much. You have to relax and have more time for yourself.

Phil: You're right. Tomorrow I don't have to work, so I'll sleep late!

Expressions

fall asleep   *to sleep or start to sleep*
Phil doesn't want to **fall asleep** in the office because
he is so busy.
The baby cried all night. She just couldn't **fall
asleep**.

lie down   *to recline, to place oneself
                   in a flat position*
Phil can't **lie down** on the couch because he has to
go to a meeting.
If you have a bad headache, why don't you **lie down**
for a while?

sit down   *to be seated*
Phil and the interviewer **sit down** in the office and
continue talking.
After we shopped all day, it was nice to **sit down** in a
coffee shop and relax.

take a seat   *to sit, to be seated*
When Phil sits down, the interviewer **takes a seat** too.
Please **take a seat** in the waiting room. The doctor will see you soon.

tired out   *very tired, exhausted*
Today Phil looks **tired out**, but tomorrow he will sleep late and get rested.
You shouldn't keep on playing soccer if it **tires** you **out** so much.

EXERCISE 1

Match each idiom with its correct definition.

_____ 1. take a seat   a. very tired, exhausted

_____ 2. lie down   b. to be seated

_____ 3. fall asleep   c. to recline

_____ 4. tired out   d. to start to sleep

EXERCISE 2

Fill in each blank with the correct idiom. Each idiom is used only once.

fall asleep   lie down   sitting down
take a seat   tired out

1. I can understand why you feel _____ from working all day on your computer.
2. The doctor told the patient to _____ on his back.
3. As soon as Mary went to bed, she was able to _____.

4. Jimmy, turn that TV off! You've been
   _____ in front of it all morning!
5. Mr. Johnson will be with you in a moment. Please
   _____.

Module 4 Review

EXERCISE 1

Select the correct idiom for the boldface phrase.

1. The kitchen stove **stopped functioning** while Aaron was cooking dinner.
   a. broke down
   b. threw away
   c. kept on

2. My children **convinced me about** a trip to Disneyland during the holidays.
   a. put me off
   b. talked me into
   c. hung on to

3. Vicki **was ready** to watch TV when it suddenly broke down.
   a. got together to
   b. took a seat to
   c. was about to

4. Would you be kind enough to **assist me** with this yardwork?
   a. wear me out
   b. keep house with me
   c. help me out

5. You should **keep** those old stamps. They may be valuable some day.
   a. hang on to
   b. get rid of
   c. keep on

6. Did Jason finally **discard** that old coat he's been wearing so long?
   a. wear out
   b. throw away
   c. pick up

7. I asked Chuck if he'd like to **accompany** us to the baseball game.
   a. come along with
   b. pick up
   c. be back with

8. Can you possibly **return** to the office within two hours?
   a. get home
   b. get together
   c. be back

9. Mr. Warwick **met** and **transported** his children after school today.
   a. picked up
   b. got together
   c. came along with

10. I'm too **exhausted** from a long day at work to go out to dinner tonight.
    a. broken down
    b. tired out
    c. put off

EXERCISE 2

Fill in the boxes of the crossword puzzle with the correct idioms.

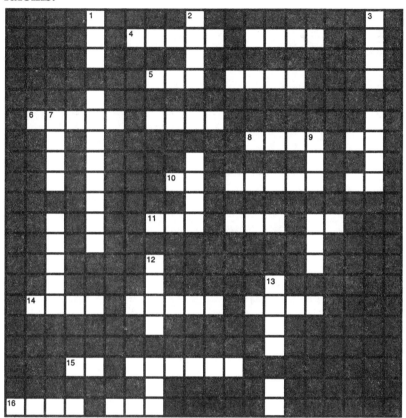

Across
4. fail to operate, stop functioning
5. recline, place oneself in a flat position
6. discard
8. continue
10. be ready or prepared to do
11. eliminate, sell
14. accompany
15. naturally, certainly
16. make or become unusable

Down
1. meet socially
2. be seated, sit
3. convince about, persuade about
7. keep, not sell or eliminate
9. postpone, delay
12. assist, aid
13. meet for the purpose of transporting

Lesson **1**

Making Repairs

Interview

The interviewer is talking to Steve Redman, owner of the local TV repair shop.

Int: Steve, my color TV set is broken. Do you think you can fix it?

Steve: Oh, sure, I can fix it. I've fixed **millions of** televisions.

Int: Good. I don't know what I'd do without my TV.

Steve: Don't worry. I've worked on this model many times. **Quite a few** sets of this type have problems.

Int: Really?

Steve: Oh, yes. Look at this new model over here. It's **topnotch**.

Int: Wow! That's a great picture. Do you have any problems with it?

Steve: Well, **so far** I've worked on only **a handful** of them, and they're very reliable. They give most people no trouble **at all**.

Int: That sounds good. Maybe I'll get one soon.

Expressions

---

a handful of   *a few of, some*
Only **a handful of** the new TV models have had any serious problems.
I thought I had plenty of money, but all I had was **a handful of** change.

at all   *to any degree*
The new TV model shouldn't cause any problems **at all**.
Lois doesn't like her boss **at all**. She thinks he's very unfair.

millions of   *countless, very many*
Steve has fixed **millions of** televisions in his job as
TV repairman.
My mother has told me **millions of** times to help out
around the house.

quite a few   *many, more than several*
Quite a few sets of the same type as the interviewer's
have had problems.
Yesterday I bought **quite a few** travel books to
prepare for my trip to Spain.

so far   *until now, until this moment*
So far Steve has worked on only a handful of the
new television sets.
Betty hasn't missed a single football game **so far** this
year.

topnotch   *of the highest quality,*
                    excellent
Steve recommends the newest TV model because it is
topnotch.
This is a **topnotch** car. It's really built well.

EXERCISE 1

Match each idiom with its correct definition.

_____ 1. so far   a. more than several

_____ 2. quite a few   b. of the highest
                                 quality

_____ 3. at all   c. countless, very
                                 many

_____ 4. millions of   d. to any degree
_____ 5. topnotch   e. until now
_____ 6. a handful of   f. a few of, some

EXERCISE 2

Fill in each blank with the correct idiom. Each idiom is used only once.

a handful of	millions of	at all
quite a few	topnotch	so far

1. I've brushed my teeth _____ times in my life; I almost never forget to do so.
2. _____ Keith has received all A's in his college courses; he's a _____ student.
3. Zena and Fred didn't like the theater presentation _____; it was boring to them.
4. _____ people speak more than one language, but only _____ them speak three or four languages.

Lesson **2**

You Never Had It so Good

Interview

The interviewer is talking to Cheryl while she is playing the piano in her home.

Int: Cheryl, you certainly **are good at** playing the piano. That's a lovely song, too.

Cheryl: Thank you. I'm glad you like it.

Int: How long have you been playing?

Cheryl: I've been studying the piano for ten years, since I was nine years old.

Int: **For goodness sake!** I didn't know that.

Cheryl: Oh, yes. Learning to play the piano is hard work, but it's all **to the good**.

Int: To the good? Do you **make money** playing the piano?

Cheryl: I didn't mean it that way, but I do make money sometimes.

Int: How?

Cheryl: I play at wedding receptions or at parties. I get paid for doing what I enjoy. **I never had it so good.**

Expressions

---

be good at   *to have a skill for*
Cheryl **is** very **good at** playing the piano.
Peter **isn't** much **good at** sports, but he loves hobbies like reading.

For goodness sake!   *Is that right! (an*
                                   exclamation of surprise)
When the interviewer learns that Cheryl has played for ten years, he responds, "**For goodness sake!**"

make money   *to earn an income*
Sometimes Cheryl is able to **make money** from her hobby.
Making money is the purpose of any business enterprise.

never had it so good   *to be in a better situation now*

Now that Cheryl can enjoy playing the piano and making money, she **never had it so good.**
After a I got a pay raise, my life became much easier. **I never had it so good.**

to the good   *to one's benefit, in profit*

All the hard work that Cheryl has done to learn the piano is all **to the good.**
After the Williams sold their house, they came out $30,000 **to the good.**

EXERCISE 1

Match each idiom with its correct definition.

_____ 1. For goodness sake!   a. to one's benefit, in profit

_____ 2. make money   b. to be in a better situation now

_____ 3. to the good   c. to earn an income

_____ 4. never had it so good   d. Is that right!

_____ 5. be good at   e. to have skill for

EXERCISE 2

Fill in each blank with the correct idiom. Each idiom is used only once.

is good at   For goodness sake!
make money   never had it so good
to the good

1. The new company was able to _____ in its first year of operation.
2. _____. There's water all over the bathroom floor!
3. Larry _____ baseball; he's the best hitter and fielder on his team.
4. The Carlsens have a luxury car, big house, and huge income; they _____.
5. After I gambled at Las Vegas, I had about $1000 _____.

Lesson **3**

Out of Order

Interview

The interviewer is talking to Marion Buckles, a mother of five children, about her hectic day.

Int:　I tried to **call** you **up** earlier today.

Marion:　Really? The telephone must be **out of order**. I'll have to get it fixed.

Int:　That's too bad.

Marion:　It sure is. But even when the phone is working, I can only talk for about a minute before I have to **hang up.** One or the other child needs help.

Int:　I can see you're **going through** a bad day.

Marion:　The worst! The children got me so **mixed up** that I missed my dental appointment. I thought the clock said two o'clock, but it was actually three o'clock. Honestly, I can't **tell time** anymore!

Expressions

call up   *to contact by phone*
The interviewer tried to **call** Marion **up** earlier in the day.
Would you **call** me **up** as soon as you get home tonight?

go through   *to endure, to experience*
He **went through** a terrible period with his illness.
Must we **go through** this again? Once was enough.

hang up   *to replace the receiver on the telephone*
Marion often has to **hang up** to take care of one of her children.
Wait! Don't **hang up**. I want to talk to Mr. Watanabe, too.

mixed up   *confused*
Sometimes Marion gets so **mixed up** that she doesn't know what time it is.

Sue got all **mixed up** on the exam and started marking the wrong answers.

out of order   *not working or functioning properly*

Marion didn't know that her telephone was **out of order**.

Don't put your money in that vending machine. The sign on it says, "**Out of order**."

tell time   *be able to read a clock or watch*

Marion is so busy with her five children that she sometimes forgets how to **tell time**.

Children are very proud when they learn how to **tell time**.

EXERCISE 1

Match each idiom with its correct definition.

_____ 1. mixed up	a. be able to read a clock or watch
_____ 2. out of order	b. to contact by phone
_____ 3. tell time	c. confused
_____ 4. hang up	d. to replace the receiver
_____ 5. call up	e. not functioning properly

EXERCISE 2

Fill in each blank with the correct idiom. Each idiom is used only once.

call up	hung up	mixed up
out of order	tell time	

1. We'll have to walk up the stairs to the fifth floor. The elevator is _____.
2. Sailors are able to _____ by checking the location of the sun.
3. I thought that the meeting was tomorrow. I'm all _____!
4. Let's _____ Jack and Ted and see if they can visit tonight.
5. Ralph let the phone ring over ten times before he _____.

Lesson **4**

Shopping and So On

Interview

The interviewer is talking to a salesman, Craig Rosen, about buying a new sports coat.

Int: How does this one look, Craig? Does it look **all right**?

Craig: It's a little too big. You should have **at least** one size smaller.

Int: I hate to shop alone. I like to have my wife with me. She has a very good sense of clothing.

Craig: True. **On second thought**, you haven't bought this one **as yet**, so it's not too late to ask her advice. Why don't you bring her later today to help you decide on the color, style, price, **and so on**.

Int: I'll **go along with** that idea, Craig. That's what I'll do.

Craig: OK. I'll see you both later.

88

Expressions

all right	*correct, satisfactory,* *OK (okay)*

The interviewer wonders if the new suit looks **all right** on him.

Is it **all right** if I smoke in this room?

and so on	*etcetera (for a continuing* *series of related items)*

The interviewer's wife can help him decide on the color, style, price, **and so on**.

At camp in the mountains we went swimming, fishing, hiking, **and so on**.

as yet	*at this point in time*

The interviewer has not bought any clothing **as yet**.

As yet I haven't been able to find the house keys I misplaced.

at least   *a minimum of, at a minimum*
The interviewer should try another suit that is **at least** one size smaller.
It's best to eat three meals each day **at least**.

go along with *to agree with, to consent to*
The interviewer **goes along with** Craig's idea to ask his wife for her advice.
Everyone in the meeting **went along with** the director's recommendations.

on second thought *after further consideration*
On second thought, the interviewer will wait until later to buy a coat.
On second thought, I think that I will have another piece of pizza.

EXERCISE 1

Match each idiom with its correct definition.

_____ 1. go along with	a. after further consideration
_____ 2. at least	b. correct, satisfactory
_____ 3. on second thought	c. to agree with, to consent to
_____ 4. all right	d. a minimum of, at a minimum
_____ 5. as yet	e. etcetera
_____ 6. and so on	f. at this point in time

EXERCISE 2

Fill in each blank with the correct idiom. Each idiom is used only once.

| all right | on second thought | and so on |
| at least | goes along with | as yet |

1. There must have been _____ one hundred people there.

2. Is it _____ if Dora _____ us to the store?

3. I'd better leave now. Well, _____, I'll stay for a while longer.

4. _____ Todd hasn't finished school, but he will next year.

5. At the shopping center I bought new shoes, socks, pants, _____.

Module 5 Review

EXERCISE 1

Select the correct idiom for the boldface phrase.

1. It's been a long time since we've eaten in such **an excellent** restaurant!
   a. a topnotch
   b. a mixed up
   c. an all right

2. How many times have you seen that movie **until now?**
   a. and so on
   b. at all
   c. so far

3. Sarah **has a special skill for** ballet; she's the best in her class.
   a. makes money at
   b. never had it so good at
   c. is good at

4. It's never a waste of time to read books; it's all **to your benefit.**
   a. to the good
   b. mixed up
   c. for goodness sake

5. I'd like to talk to mother too! Don't **replace the receiver** yet.
   a. call up
   b. hang up
   c. go along

6. The gas pump is **not functioning**, so you'll have to move to another.
   a. all right
   b. out of order
   c. never had it so good

7. The accident occurred because the old man was **confused** by the traffic signals.
   a. on second thought
   b. at least
   c. mixed up

8. **More than several** people left the party because it was so boring.
   a. Quite a few
   b. As yet
   c. And so on

9. **A minimum of** ten people are needed for the class to be offered this term.
   a. A handful of
   b. At least
   c. Quite a few

10. **After further consideration**, I've decided to take a vacation next month.
    a. And so on
    b. So far
    c. On second thought

EXERCISE 2

Fill in the boxes of the crossword puzzle with the correct idioms.

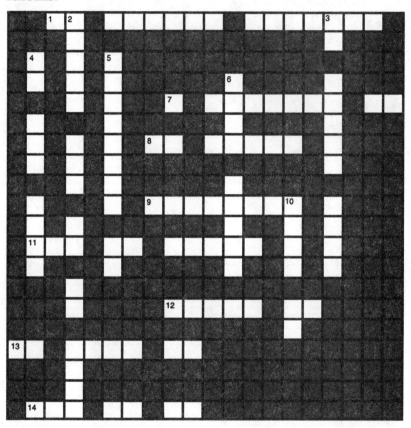

Across
1. after, further consideration
7. a few of, some
8. a minimum of, at a minimum
9. excellent, or the highest quality
11. not working or functioning properly
12. confused
13. have a skill for

Down
2. be in a better situation now
3. agree with, consent to
4. to one's benefit, in profit
5. countless, very many
6. earn an income
10. replace the reciever on the telephone

Answer Key

Module 1, Lesson 1

Exercise 1

1. b   to photograph
2. e   to give attention to
3. d   to guard against
4. f   to depend on
5. c   to make a videotape
6. a   to examine

Exercise 2

1. shoots a video
2. takes a picture of
3. look at
4. watch out for
5. see about
6. looked to

Module 1, Lesson 2

Exercise 1

1. e   to discuss
2. a   to pay attention to
3. c   to appreciate
4. d   to request
5. f   to consult
6. b   to know about

Exercise 2

1. goes in for
2. asked for
3. heard of
4. listens to
5. speak to
6. talk about

Module 1, Lesson 3

Exercise 1

1. d   to sample
2. c   in an obvious place
3. a   conceited
4. e   accurately
5. b   to continue

Exercise 2

1. had a taste of
2. went n
3. laughed at
4. on the nose
5. stuck-up

Module 1, Lesson 4

Exercise 1

1. d   to be remembered
2. f   eventually
3. e   to calculate
4. a   to have an opinion about
5. b   to indicate
6. c   to produce

Exercise 2

1. pointed out
2. figure out
3. think of
4. came up with
5. comes to mind
6. in the long run

Module 1 Review

Exercise 1

1. b   look at
2. a   watch out for
3. b   ask for
4. a   listen to
5. c   speak to
6. c   right under my nose
7. a   laugh at
8. b   had a taste of
9. a   figure out
10. a   come up with

Exercise 2

Module 2, Lesson 1

Exercise 1

1. d   to approach closely
2. b   to visit
3. a   to compromise with
4. c   to recognize by appearance
5. e   to use a given name

Exercise 2

1. call on
2. call you by your first name
3. know...by sight
4. meet...halfway
5. come up to

Module 2, Lesson 2

Exercise 1

1. e   comfortable, relaxed
2. a   to respect
3. b   by memorizing completely
4. c   to gradually accept
5. d   to live or work well with

Exercise 2

1. get used to
2. look up to
3. by heart
4. get along with
5. at ease

Module 2, Lesson 3

Exercise 1

1. e   to end a relationship with
2. c   to recover from
3. a   to date regularly
4. d   to become in love with
5. b   to disappoint

Exercise 2

1. going with him
2. let her down
3. break up with
4. fall for it
5. getting over

Module 2, Lesson 4

Exercise 1

1. b   to surrender
2. d   to fulfill
3. c   directly, personally
4. a   had the habit or custom to
5. e   to be completed or finished

Exercise 2

1. give up
2. was over
3. face to face
4. live up to
5. used to

Module 2 Review

Exercise 1

1. b   call him by his first name
2. a   come up to them
3. b   call on you
4. c   getting used to
5. b   at ease
6. c   let her down
7. c   get over
8. b   going with
9. c   give up
10. a   live up to

Exercise 2

Module 3, Lesson 1

Exercise 1

1. e   nervous, anxious
2. d   occasionally
3. f   to benefit, to help
4. b   to enjoy oneself
5. c   temporarily
6. a   repeatedly, frequently

Exercise 2

1. time and time again
2. having a good time
3. doing you good
4. for the time being
5. on edge
6. at times.

Module 3, Lesson 2

Exercise 1

1. b   gradually
2. c   hurried, rushed
3. a   repeatedly
4. d   permanently, forever
5. e   customarily

Exercise 2

1. as usual
2. in a hurry
3. little by little
4. over and over
5. for good

Module 3, Lesson 3

Exercise 1

1. c   throughout the day
2. a   in the beginning
3. e   during one's entire lifetime
4. b   suddenly
5. f   absolutely not
6. d   sometimes

Exercise 2

1. not on your life
2. all her life
3. from time to time
4. all of a sudden
5. all week long
6. at first

Module 3, Lesson 4

Exercise 1

1. c   to create space for
2. a   very quickly, rapidly
3. e   occasionally
4. d   to be expired
5. f   to raise from childhood
6. b   to attend school

Exercise 2

1. make room for
2. going to college
3. in no time
4. bringing up
5. now and then
6. was up

Module 3 Review

Exercise 1

1. b   do you good
2. c   for the time being
3. b   on edge
4. b   as usual
5. c   over and over
6. a   little by little
7. b   all her life
8. a   all night long
9. a   now and then
10. b   in no time

Exercise 2

Module 4, Lesson 1

Exercise 1

1. e   to fail to operate
2. a   to convince, to persuade
3. d   to postpone, to delay
4. c   to continue
5. b   to be ready or prepared to

Exercise 2

1. put it off
2. was about to
3. talk her into
4. broke down
5. keep on

Module 4, Lesson 2

Exercise 1

1. b   to discord
2. c   to do the necessary housework
3. d   to assist, to aid
4. f   to keep, not to sell
5. a   to make or become unusable
6. e   to eliminate, to sell

Exercise 2

1. get rid of
2. throw away
3. keep house
4. help out
5. hang on to
6. wore out

Module 4, Lesson 3

Exercise 1

1. b   to meet socially
2. d   to arrive home
3. f   to accompany
4. e   to return somewhere
5. c   to meet to transport
6. a   naturally, certainly

Exercise 2

1. got home
2. be back
3. come along with
4. pick up
5. got together
6. of course

Module 4, Lesson 4

Exercise 1

1. b   to be seated
2. c   to recline
3. d   to start to sleep
4. a   very tired, exhausted

Exercise 2

1. tired out
2. lie down
3. fall asleep
4. sitting down
5. take a seat

Module 4 Review

Exercise 1

1. a   broke down
2. b   talked me into
3. c   was about to
4. c   help me out
5. a   hang on to
6. b   throw away
7. a   come along with
8. c   be back
9. a   picked up
10. b   tired out

Exercise 2

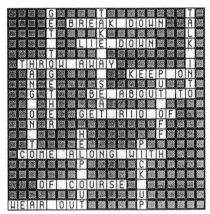

Module 5, Lesson 1

Exercise 1

1. e   until now
2. a   more than several
3. d   to any degree
4. c   countless, very many
5. b   of the highest quality
6. f   a few of, some

Exercise 2

1. millions of
2. so far/topnotch
3. at all
4. quite a few/a handful of

Module 5, Lesson 2

Exercise 1

1. d   Is that right!
2. c   to earn an income
3. a   to one's benefit, in profit
4. b   to be in a better situation now
5. e   to have skill for

Exercise 2

1. make money
2. For goodness sake!
3. is good at
4. never had it so good
5. to the good

Module 5, Lesson 3

Exercise 1

1. c   confused
2. e   not functioning properly
3. a   be able to read a clock
4. d   to replace the receiver
5. b   to contact by phone

Exercise 2

1. out of order
2. tell time
3. mixed up
4. call up
5. hung up

Module 5, Lesson 4

Exercise 1

1. c   to agree with, to consent to
2. d   a minimum of, at a minimum
3. a   after further consideration
4. b   correct, satisfactory
5. f   at this point in time
6. e   etcetera

Exercise 2

1. at least
2. all right/goes along with
3. on second thought
4. As yet
5. and so on

Module 5 Review

Exercise 1

1. a   a topnotch
2. c   so far
3. c   is good at
4. a   to the good
5. b   hang up
6. b   out of order
7. c   mixed up
8. a   quite a few
9. b   at least
10. c   on second thought

Exercise 2

```
 O N   S E C O N D   T H O U G H T
   E                           O
 T U M               M         A
 O E I               M         A
   R L   A   H A N D F U L   O F
 T L K                       O
 H H I   A T   L E A S T     N
 E A L                       G
 O N     M
 G S   T O P N O T C H   U
 O I               N   A   I
 O U T   O F   O R D E R   N T
 D   F             Y   G H
     S
     O         M I X E D   U P
                         P
 B E   G O O D   A T
   O
   O
 A N D   S O   O N
```

Index

Note: The pages indicated are where the idioms first appear in this book.